T0128490

POEMS, RHYMES & REAL

HEARTFELT STUFF

GEORGE TEDESCO

authorHOUSE

AuthorHouse™
1663 Liberty Drive
Bloomington, IN 47403
www.authorhouse.com
Phone: 1 (800) 839-8640

Published by AuthorHouse 04/21/2020

ISBN: 978-1-7283-5979-3 (sc)
ISBN: 978-1-7283-5978-6 (e)

Print information available on the last page.

Table of Contents

Introduction

To the readers and fans of the poem book series;

thank you for all the encouraging words and positive feedback. And because of such, I am proud to release this fourth book to continue this wonderful collection of finely written, bathroom reading material.

Each book has it's own delivery and style, this one is unique as well in that it is curse free. A no swearing poem book, anyone can read, anywhere! For example; in an airport, or church, or on line at Walmart, if Walmart shoppers could read. Just saying, you could literally read this anywhere. In space? Perhaps. Try it, then let me know.

A wise man once said to me behind a dumpster,

"I don't need the best dog food, I just need something to feed the dog."

Okay, so he was more of a free-thinking dumpster diver than a wise man, but he could've been wise, we don't know for sure. The point is, it sounded good and I'm going to apply that thinking here. I'm not trying to compete with history's best poets, I simply made some dog food. Just try to swallow it.

After four poem books I feel like I now have the time to share that I am also a singer, songwriter, and guitarist of the band GLAZIA. It's something I never thought I'd hear myself admitting as a heavy metal guitarist; that I enjoy writing poems, but I do. In fact, some of the poems in these books are *my* songs, or variations of.

That being said, with all the technology of today and the availability of super apps helping song writers and poets in their endeavors, it can be difficult sifting through the trash finding what's real and heartfelt, intelligently and purposely written, clever and witty or what's manufactured through "apps". So yes, these programs are absolutely 100%

appalling to someone like myself who write with mood and feeling, along with inner creativity and life experiences as inspiration.

If an app or program is showing me seventy-five rhymes, synonyms and phrases I could use, I feel like that kind of defeats the entire purpose of creative expression through your level of capability, whether in music or poetry.

I find it challenging and interesting to write with wider or softer rhymes. In other words, all the rhymes may not have that exact letter or syllable structure like 'fatter' and 'matter'. (Sure, sometimes I will rhyme tight) but in some cases I prefer not to as it is a heck of a lot more challenging rhyming with wider reaching words. It'll still have that rhyme feel and still give you that resolve that lets you move on, just not so fifth grade. Same goes for sentence structure, since I'm not using the typical stanza format. But again, there is a flow and beat or rhythmic design that will deliver you to the next thought down the line.

I've thoroughly enjoyed creating my own personal style and equally enjoyed meeting the challenges of writing. Whether it be of the short story type poem or the slam poetry type, the heartfelt soul-baring poem or the more uplifting, motivational ones, I love the books I've created. They are all me, my heart, my mind and my soul, written purely for my own personal enjoyment that I decided to share and I truly hope you find happiness within the passages. If not, you cannot have your money back. I already spent it.

I wrote this during the Corona-virus pandemic and I was one of the lucky ones who got back on my feet after getting the virus. My condolences, love and respect go out to the families who lost loved ones during this tragic time. God bless everyone and stay safe.

*   Poems, Rhymes & Real Heartfelt Sh*t

**   Poems, Passages & Real Heartfelt Sh*t

***   Poems, Rhymes & Real Foul Mouthed Sh*t

****   Poems, Rhymes & Real Heartfelt Stuff

A Heart's Reply

Through days of pain
I wonder why I'm awake.
I've slept through sunny days, starlit nights and
beautiful mornings, but for the pain, it seems,
I'm always awake.
Today is one of those days I ask that question...
And then my heart replied,

*"You don't want to sleep through the pain. It's rare
and stands for something greater than the day.
It's only considered pain, because it's a deeply
cherished 'Love' we're saying goodbye to.
But our tears vouch for the memories we hold onto
and will never let go of.
Pain will eventually wash away and fade
from the rains of time,
leaving only that 'Love' to remain
and stay inside our hearts and minds."*

Built to Rust

I'm tired of being locked up inside my mind,
hiding behind fake smiles, pretending
I'm just fine, watching time fly by while
others control the flow of my life.
It's a pathetic existence to whine.
It's even more pathetic to have lived your
life without putting up a fight.
Crying never saved a life or steered a ship in the night.
Actions have always spoke louder than words,
but these words need to be heard.
I know what's inside me and
I'm more than what this world has let me be.
I've proven myself time and again and yet here I stand,
a worthless piece of magnificent machinery.

Entranced

It amazes me how long I can stare into her eyes,
how much I crave for us to be alone and next to her
at night.
The more my eyes fall softly on her,
the more I adore the entirety of her.
Her eyes, her hair, her goodbyes, her beautiful stare.
Her voice and smile, carry me for days and miles.
Her hands and lips, her willingness to kiss.
Her facial expressions, her laughter,
the way she... exists.

Unforgettable

Her kiss envelopes you, just as oceans of
meadowbloom do to the honeybees in June.
Her perfume, sweet and delicious just as the fresh Georgia
peach's fragrance is enchantingly malicious, mentally
promiscuous, intoxicating and promising, while dancing
through your thoughts as you exhaustingly search
to find new things to say to separate the animalistic
way you want to prey on her beauty, such as the way
she instantaneously erases history or the sparks she
creates when she enters a room becoming your fantasy,
fanning the flames of your intertwined destiny.
I've lost myself in that beauty.

Her eyes say to stay, not for the night, but forever.
They tell stories of love and tenderness, unforgettable
nights of bliss to be discovered when you connect
in that kiss, resurrecting love that had been sent to
lie dormant in your hearts long before you both
met.

Convenient Faith

Heavily onto stone you fall.
Sorrow raked deep into bone and soul.
Your darkest moment, your darkest hour.
Emptiness engulfs as you slowly unravel.
Torn apart at the seems by your own arrogance.
You now believe in reprieve and a second chance.
No need to pray.
Ignored and forsaken?
or undeserved and sadly mistaken.

<u>Escape</u>

Coursing like virus through vein,
the deepest part of your being, restrained,
electric energy, internally connecting, spirit and bone,
the crave that wants to howl at the moon,
has been chained down and drowned,
unexpectedly, you're entombed.

Your voice needs to be heard.
You want to scream til it hurts.
You're buried so far underneath
what everyone else believes,
you don't even know, how to be free of the curse,
much less feed your inner beast what it deserves.
Time is running out.
You must find the real you and find the way out.

<u>Sweet Dreams</u>

Goodnight little one.
Relax. Breathe easy and let yourself gently
fall deep asleep into sweet dreams.

I'm now realizing a new baby couldn't
possibly have anything to dream about,
so let me help

Dream of my arms holding you when you're
tired, cold and scared.

Dream of my voice guiding you through every
rough day and every nightmare.

Dream of me giving you all the encouragement
and all the tools you'll ever need
to be inspired and succeed.

I'll always defend you.
I'll never turn my back on you
and I'll give you all the love your little heart can hold.

Welcome to this world.

Wise Man Said

Life is scary.
I've never known it not to be.
Meeting people for the first time.
Being broke and hungry.
Falling in love.
Embarking on a new journey.
Being far away from home.
Holding your new baby.
Being naked in front of someone.
A doctor saying maybe.
Confrontations.
Stranded and alone.
Praying to an entity you've never known.
Battling sickness that could kill us.
Trying.
Being homeless.
Death and dying.
Watching your children suffer.
Losing the TV remote in the sofa.

Bittersweet Tomorrow

Clocks turn, counting down the hours.
Life burns, like floating ash embers,
but you remember,
moments in time
have vanished in the blink of an eye,
instantly becoming memories sold to yesterday
without saying goodbye.

With friends now buried and a child now grown,
what purpose does a memory have besides reminding
me of a life that I once loved and lived so long ago.

It's a miserable reminder haunting my mind
like a painful shadow, creeping up behind,
constantly with me, jabbing me, saddening me.
I've tried to just let go of the pain,
I've cried and screamed at the sorrow,
but those memories remain, while getting
further away with each new tomorrow.

Burn to the last

Burn to the last drop of gas in the tank.
Burn the wick down to the glass bottom
on which it sits.
Create a disturbance, be the ruckus,
but keep your focus,
for when the clock strikes and the hand asks for yours,
You can go willingly, happily knowing you forged
fires that'll keep burning long after you're gone,
keeping others warm, lighting their way.
Burn to the last match, using every
chance you had to light that blaze.
Burn til the last drop of blood stops moving
and dries in your veins.
Burn like a rocket might
proving it's more than just a test flight.
God gave you time to play.
So, play. Play with fire and become your desire.
Burn higher. *Burn* richer.
Scorch the earth on which you stand,
til there's no regrets and no more plans.

Scars

The haunting souvenirs of regret,
born out of darkness, become part of us.
They can exist skin deep, or way down in our core.
Let down or led astray, lied to or abandoned,
cut by wretched tongue or sharpened blade,
the wounds they leave
burden our being with a painful memory
that have altered our form.
No endeavor, sickness, journey, marriage or war
has ever left a man unmarred.
Whether heartbroken or battle torn, he'll
leave reminded of what he's endured.
A man scarred is a man learned.
They're a part of life.
To carry them means... you survived.

Playing with Fire

How could I have been so foolishly dim. Enamored with
glamour like an animal drawn to a shiny lure within.
I've always been able to see right through her thin veil
of deception and lies and yet I continued to ignore
the signs of a terribly shallow, selfish being inside.

What's wrong with me that I lost step with the concept
of protecting and preserving one self. I'm dying to know
why I abandoned my own soul, forfeit my own goals
and left, not just parts, but all of me, out in the cold.
I mean, I know why, and I should've let go, long ago.

If only I could speak to the old me, I'd tear down
those childish dreams and fantasies, because in
reality and believe me, it seems spectacular, but it
can be a catastrophe, like playing with a cunning
flame that grows everytime you breathe. I'd beg me
to leave the scene before I got burned with nowhere
left to go, scorched and alone with nothing but an
empty hole from where a thief stole my soul.

Transport

Water falls over limestone walls,
cascading over hanging gardens of moss.
Birds reset their nests on well chosen branches
while the sun soaks the day with its warmth.
Brightly colored creatures swim and breed with
elegance underneath the tepid stream's shimmer.
Nature is finally back, and having her
way after the long brutal winter.
For a moment, trapped in bird's song, it seemed
as though the earth stopped spinning, time
unexisted as a serenity met the humming ambiance
of the floral adorned, tree-lined river.

This is the calm my mind insisted I find
to release the days dark linger.
To think of a beautiful place, I could escape and
rather be, than this God forsaken hell I'm living.

Toxicity

Breathe in the toxicity.
Choke on the the noxious ignorance.
Feel the stubbornness and lack of elasticity.
See the obnoxious impatience, the unnecessarily
abrasive, over defensive, over aggressive,
hands up, it's not my problem, disease.
Anyone can complain. Anyone can claim it's not me.
If every man stood on the same side of the boat,
it would sink into the sea.

Turns out, there is an "I" in team. It stands for I think
I'LL finally stop selfishly ignoring the ones around me.
I think I'LL finally be more than just a man walking
around this world's obvious needs. I think I'LL be a
part of the world that needs me to be more than just
me and I'LL stop contributing to the world's toxicity.

Doors & Floors

You can wake up one morning
and be shown the way to the door.
I've been homeless many times
and I'm sure I will be many more.
Sometimes we don't see eye to eye,
sometimes your world crumbles on the inside.

You can pray, you can say
you can do anything you want,
but it won't change the fact
that you're only human, which means
there's room for movement, including losing,
and it's okay to be good at that.

No time for crying, no whining, just hear me out.
No matter how much money you invest,
time you put in or think you've beaten the test
or put your best foot in,
this life may just, not want you to win.

So I decided to go with the flow, and thank
the universe for all the open doors it gave me,
and all the floors that saved me,
an exciting life, that's different all the time,
a few friends, some family
and the possibility of maybe,
is good enough for me.

<u>Lantern</u>

I walk in darkness.
Any light I could've used has been
overshadowed by past and pain.
I don't know why my life had to be this way, so
tiring, so lonely, so annoyingly cliche,
but it has happened
again and again.
This tunnel I brave has me on edge
as I'm scared of what's to come and
what the hell could be next.
I can't see the end, for all I know it could smack
me right in the face in the next few steps.
I've been lucky with friends,
they've helped me get back on my feet,
back, pretty much where I needed to be,
but after the smiles and goodbyes,
I'm left with just this road and me.

They say God walks with you, whispering the
strengths you'll need to use. That may be so, however
more often than not, I've made the wrong move.

Suddenly out of the blue,
I felt this presence, walking, then running,
faintly calling- as if the voice knew.
To shine a light on what I stopped believing in,
to show me the way out of the blackened sewer
I'd been wading through.
The dim light got brighter as it drew near.
The voice got louder and a little more clear.
It was a woman I'd never met, calling my name.
Trust me, I was just as shocked as you.

So amazingly beautiful, so sincere and true.
She was to be the love of my life, sent to find me,
help guide me, and walk by my side,
as my heavenly lantern of light.

Rockstar

I stood there and watched the room fall silent.
I watched the world come to a crawl.
On it's seat, waiting for me to breathe and then before
I could blink, or even think,
the world watched me bare my soul.
I sang and I strummed my guitar in that special
way only I could, and I played my heart out in a
song I wrote long before that amazing day stood.
The world was in shock, I was in awe as they fell to their
knees, moved, cheering, loving all that I had done,
all that I worked so hard to become.
I couldn't be more proud of myself.
I don't even know what to say.
except...
It never went down that way. I've played my guitar for
thirty years and never got off the small stage.
My life hit the skids, I had some kids and before
I knew it, it was too late, I'm now forty eight.
I guess its true what they say; chase those dreams
hard or you'll surely regret it one day,
possibly on your birthday.

Her Hands

Just your everyday tools of the trade you say.
Just plain old hands to do the
mundane chores they're made for,
but to the world around you, they're so much more.
Take *my* hand and follow me through this door.

I've watched you feed your babies and tickle smiles
deep into their souls. Pick them up when they're
sick and coddle them when they're cold.
I've seen you carry your workload home so
you can pay the bills that swarm,
but of course they don't and all the children
know is, Mommy, keeps us fed and warm.

You're an amazing mother with an amazing touch,
And at the end of the day, your hands still find a way
to make me feel loved.
You caress my face and rub my back, you touch
me in ways, my heart could never re-pay.
The fact is, your hands have steered a ship so
steadily through every storm, that no one aboard
has the slightest notion
they're traversing a most treacherous ocean.

Relentless

Relentless is her beauty...
and I can explain. I'm not just going to write a passage
about a girl because I think she's beautiful, that's
insane. It's immature, and I don't play those kind of
games. Of course she's special because she's mine,
but why she's beautiful is what I want to explain.
That's all I'm trying to say.

And now I feel rushed and uncomfortable and
honestly? Maybe I shouldn't talk about my girl
this way since you're so demanding, over bearing,
unrelenting, possibly even critical. Which is terrible,
just awful, disgraceful, distasteful, and rude.
To tell you the truth, I think this friendship has ran
its course. Seriously man, you're the worst, dude.

The Key

There once was a door and behind it
existed a life I truly needed.
For this I held a key.

Whilst in the other hand, I held my dreams;
a wishful, unrealistic grandeur
where my mind wandered.
For this, there was only uncertainty.

Why then, did I choose to chase what cannot be,
instead of using the key to a better reality?
Hindsight is always 20/20.
It's painful to let go and abandon the seed of your
being, the inner drive of desire and achievement,
but realistically, the dream was never going to feed my
soul. It was a light that lived deep within shadow.

Finding another door is all that matters to me,
and I think I still have that old key.

Renegotiate

Can we be more than what we bargained for?
What if we didn't know we,
individually, were worth more?
So you got beat down and settled on a level where
you accepted this stifle as the furthest you'd travel,
and now you're begging to be free, but you're locked
into the mediocrity that has shackled your own
destiny to the planks of 'where you'll never be'.
You can cry and whine
or wake up and break those chains that have you bound
to the line of bricks that are sinking you and your ship.
I say, renegotiate those bargaining chips.

Resist

Resist to engage
Detest the rage.
Put to rest the question whether or not
your even going to entertain the insane.
They feed on hate and other's pain.
Shutdown what must be.
Ignore the masses that deplete your energy.
Remember, misery loves company.
Cut off what feeds the enemy.

The Inside

Piece by piece, night after night,
you assemble the being that you want to see
in the mirror.
You avoid doing things to your body
that could cause harm
or even appear as false charm.
Yet you forgot one thing...

The inside.

Where darkness and demons lie.
You've polished the outside so divine,
spending so much time on how
attractive you'll be found,
you've overlooked the most important of part...

Your heart.

Not your actual heart, the internal part that declares
your worth. The part that extends compassion
and empathy, strong enough not to envy,
resisting greed, deception and jealousy.
Embrace who you are and all that you can be.
Just don't forget the inside, the place you cannot see...

That's the true key to humanity.

<u>Winter's Last Breath</u>

Blue flows through white,
as white fades into blue.
Wheat grass peeks out of snow drifts,
as food in the Alaskan bloom.
Quiet crackling forests covered in frozen droplets,
slowly melt and turn into mountain streams,
announcing it's time to start a new.

Awaken does the day,
as the sun starts it's seasonal thaw.
An eagle's lone cry soars high in the bright skies above.
Through frosty air he glides,
spreading his wings in the wind stream
where he resides,
telling winter to take it's last breath and
say it's final goodbye.

End of Days

Take your share,
and bite the hand that feeds you.
Say, you care, as long as no one speaks.
Fake your praise, your lies have helped your gain.
Collide, divide, there is no end in sight.

Show me your worth, as you bathe in blood.
Break your word, you walk the line absurd.
You steal your turn.
Manipulation first,
to get what you deserve.

you'll get what you deserve.

Eyes ever so wide, watch in disgrace,
we are delivering heaven to hell.
Anthems revised, chantings of change.
We have fallen before the race.
Time is a fault line, lying in wait,
to crumble us in to our graves.
We are one, we are strong,
but we've lost all control.

I don't want to change your mind,
or waste our time
with your fake apologies.
I just wanna fill you in on the change,
for you, these are the
End of Days.

Stubborn Fool

So stubborn was the fool,
stubborn as the mule,
he refused to change or accept he had
a narrow point of view.

Opportunities passed,
sadness amassed and loneliness began
to envelope his soul.
"A better way exists", claimed his friends.
Salvation and bliss mixed with riches,
can make you feel whole.
It's literally within reaching distance."

But did the fool listen?
Did he change his tune or learn his lesson,
or try something else besides the misdirection
his stubbornness has led him?

<u>Creative Writing 101</u>

Writing on the whole is writing from the soul.
It's writing in your own style,
your own wheelhouse of production.
It's your own version of a personally stamped concoction.
It's recollection, dissection, redirection and
resurrection of your past, being brought to life,
encapsulated in phrases,
in spaces on pages that are the canvases of the
stages of success and failures you portray.
So paint away, create the words that
sew the seams that want to fray.
Make and mold your poems as if
they were made of clay.
And don't be afraid of what others will think.
It's none of their business anyway.

Blank Stare

Sky hides inside her mind, flashing a phony smile.
sipping her tea while dining with the
person she's been dating awhile.
Ho-hum goes the conversation,
shes completely bored of their union.
With concern and care, her trance gaze
was sensed and mentioned.
"Once again, you're in a haze, there's that
blank stare." her lover said in frustration.
"Tell me what's wrong.
"Maybe there's something I can do to fix it."

Sky wasn't looking to mend their situation
and wasn't sharing her decision,
she was just waiting for the right time to end it.

Years go by before she does, all because
it was never about love,
but something else she wanted to make sure of.
A shock to the system, it was
for Angel, who never knew what hit her
when Skylar finally told her;

"Our best nights are over.
It's time for you to go, I've replaced you
with someone else's shoulder,
Thanks for... whatever."

Angel was devastated, heartbroken and shattered.
her heart in pieces that she no longer mattered.
She had loved Skylar so deeply, for so long.

"If only there were signs" she said in mourn.

Moonlit

A little girl once loved the moon
so much, she asked her dad to lift
her up so she could touch it.
"It's not that simple", he replied, "but I promise,
if I can find a way to bend the sky before I die,
I'll make the moon follow you every night."

Then one clear night he woke his little girl
out of a sound sleep.
He whispered, "I did it, but it's a secret
you'll have to swear, you'll keep."
She happily agreed as he carried her into the car.
He told her to look out the window,
so he could show her what he had done so far
in keeping the promise he made her heart.

The little girl's face lit up with joy
as the moon filled her eyes like a magical new toy.
She smiled for miles as she watched the moon follow
her down every road they traveled that night.
"Thank you Daddy" she happily sighed.

Warrior

Weary, the warrior stood,
leaning to one side with tired breath.
"You all look at me- as if I have answers.
Well, maybe some." he said.

"Wounds of the heart bore deep into our being.
Our souls become stricken, and bleed past feeling.
We harden with sorrow, slip away into darkness
and slowly stop believing in ourselves
and the hopes of tomorrow.

"Make no mistake,"
he said, pulling his sword from it's sheath.
"Battles will be faced. Sacrifices will be made.
You'll be war-torn and reeling,
but never forget you survived such a fight and
the deepest cuts, require the longest healing."

Sacred

I've been around long enough to get,
all of demons in closets in your head.
I think about about all the things you said,
it's only the pain I feel you'll regret.

Of course there's a long road up ahead,
but it's filled with the things you'd never expect.
They say there's a reason we get what we get,
and maybe, just maybe, it'll work in the end.

Hear me,
before it all turns faded.
We can find a way to understand.
If not your life then tell me what is sacred,
you can't tell me this is where we belong.

I can see that your cornered in your mind,
all alone and you can't feel what is right.
You carry your sorrow and your fears,
with the weight of the world, inside your tears.
I beg you to hold on.
They'll be days when the sun will rise again.
Don't give in to the cold numb.
It's just the pain that wants to pull you in.

Wise Man Said II

We mistakenly weigh our worth
on what we think we need;
a person by our side to validate our strides,
fame and fortune, or
the success of our dreams.

It's funny, because none of these
define who we are.
In our rawest form with our purest potential
we are the moments we create
with whom we care for.
The rest is just a distraction of the superficial.

On the Edge

Standing on the edge
of what, I'm not sure, cliff or blade,
don't really know just yet, but I'm back to this place
I've been many times before.

Life... is reality. It's not a separate being.
It doesn't have vindictive policy, competing dreams
or even feelings. It's a flow of our time combined
with our decisions, that make up our lives.
And in this reality we call "life",
I'm somehow back on the edge of what now seems
a blade, for conversation sake,
painfully balancing the reality of loss and gain,
the life I've made
and the future of change.
Here I go again.

Friends

Darkest hours shine the most light.
They expose who's worth
your love, energy and time.
Never let negativity over power your peace of mind.
Even just one bad thought, eventually, can be your demise.
Everyone's a friend through thick.
It's the ones who hang around through thin
that deserve your greatest respect.
Keep a close eye on them all, even kin,
for one day they may either need to be shown the door
or picked up, like they did for you,
when they hit the floor.

Brightside of Dark

Round we go, in motion like carousels,
laughing, loving, holding hands, like paintings in halls.
Screaming at the ocean, while skimming purple stones,
we recognize there's something special,
to good to let go.

Yet, with all we know,
you think we'd get along.
If you're always right and I know how I feel,
then who's wrong in this slowly darkening,
forever disheartening, once enveloping,
now downward spiraling dream?

It's good we walked away when we did,
I can still see your smiles.
If we waited any longer, there would have been
a trail of tears for miles.

Realign II

Channeled cries within your mind,
they terrify.
Off the chosen path you've fallen,
can't deny.
Your inner voice is calling to calm and rectify.
It's only a matter of time
before we all die.

Realize. Realign.
The moment you feel everything just slip away,
Rewrite. Realign.
The moment you feel you'll never see the light of day,
change your ways and realign your life.

The answer lies within your fight,
close your eyes,
and silence every demon that consumes your life.
Your inner voice is calling to calm and rectify.
listen to it.
And

Realize. Realign.

Precious Cost

Sorrowful cries of the heart
from sincerity's depths,
beg not to be torn apart.
Can love exist without a price?
Our souls crave love and need it to survive.
To love and be loved.
It's who we are from birth to grave.
It's the whole purpose we're made.
We chase the love we want, fight hard to find it, nurture
it, caress it, even sit on the end of beds and pray for it.
If you have never known what it's like to have
cried in the dark, on your knees, for a love you've lost,
then you may not understand it's
extremely rare precious cost.

Explorer

Gases amaze through colorful haze,
as pin pricked lights pepper the dark night.
Surrounded by space, no man can explain,
we rocket through the cosmos in search of new life.

As constellations guide, we comb the distant skies
at speeds beyond comprehension and time.
We coast through this tranquil sea of nothingness
with nothing less than the eagerness to survive.

We check our facts and figures, measurements
and instruments, and calculate destinations
and possibilities with our equipment.
We'll rise to meet the challenges of our lives
and solve the problems we'll find.
We are the future. We are the remarkable.
We are the dreamers of mankind.

At least we are, in my mind.

We are not Equals

Is it really such preposterous notion for you
to know the boundaries of your ocean?
To know the limits on how far you can intrude?
You've assumed in all your infinite wisdom
to know me and all I've been through.
You've addressed me as you would individuals who
expect life to hand feed them in a world where
many of us had to bleed for them.

Equals?? No, we are not equals.
We could never be. Not that it matters, and
not that I would've treated you differently,
but since you brought it up.
You haven't gone through what I've had to
just to be able to sit down and breathe.
You want to be considered my equal?
Wake up every singe day and lose every
single thing you've every loved.
Do that for decades, day in and day out.
Go toe to toe with misery bout for bout.
then tell me what you think life is about.

You can sit by my side and watch the tides,
we can share meals and laugh together through time,
but parts of me have lived and died.
I've lost track of the tears I've cried
and buried friends, family and dreams alike.
Don't dare to think you know my type.

Priceless

As the world slowly became distant and dim,
doesn't matter why,
war, corruption, sickness or sin,
I looked around and all I could see
was what's unimportant in the grand scheme of things.

As I lay there, alone,
shaking with fever, aching in every way,
I saw how my collection of this and that
couldn't save me from a spec of misery and pain.
My trinkets and jewelry couldn't bring me
water or food,
nor could they pull up my blankets and warm the room.

What matters most became perfectly clear
when the world's lights went out this year.

Failing to Live

So many regrets, so many failed attempts,
do I dare entertain the thought to venture
another quest, another potential mess?
Well, it's not success that define who we are.
At best, it's failure that teaches us the most.
Failure creates drive, drive creates trying,
trying means you're alive,
striving to hand craft a victorious life.
It's getting back up after you've fallen
that makes all the difference.
It's climbing brick by brick, that builds self reliance.
It's taking a beating then deciding, not if I should
run again, but how fast should I run the next race,
instead of feeling disgraced.

So my best guess,
is the answer is always, yes.

Unstable

I'm temporarily out of service,
and closed til further notice.
I'm no longer in business and locked up
with a cease and desist on my door.
I'm abandoned and boarded up with
a hazardous unstable floor.
I'm an issued warning, trespassers beware.
I'm a systems failure, I'm offline everywhere.
I'm in need to be restored, broken down
and rebuilt from the core.
I think even before I got this virus I was a questionable
invention, unsure how I passed inspection.

Could've

Tired of hoping they'll be a better day.
Tired of thinking if only I did it this way.
Too tired to keep telling myself it matters to pray.
Too tired to pretend I'll find happiness
before my last day.
And then it dawned on me, I'm in control of me.
I'm holding out for hope to rescue me like this is
some kind of fantasy, but this is the reality I created
for me, so there's no one to blame- but me.
but if just for a minute I wanted to wonder if God
let me wander too far alone, I pondered...
and no matter how hard I tried to be bitter, there
was another moment where I'd remember,
I could've suffered worse.
I could've been alone and felt like I was cursed.
I could've been left out in the rain, in pain, without
a friend to take my hand and give me strength to
find a way to meet the challenges of a new day.
but I wasn't, and never was, for more than a moment.

So I think I'll re-adjust my thinkin', redirect my
blame and then thank the heavens for everything I'd
been given, starting with the fact that I'm livin'.
Cuz it could've been a whole lot worse.

Break Free

Life is short, here's what I've found;
It's often difficult to see what's causing us to drown.
Freeing ourselves of negativity that's around
can be as simple as
saturate and surround yourself with
those who don't bring you down.
Seems simple enough you say, but
sometimes it's the ones closest to us that need to part
ways; blood or not, if they're stopping your flow,
they're the blood clot.
It's now mandatory,
a commandment for me, no matter the complexity,
to make an example
of anybody who tries to contain me or break me.
I need to break free of other's ideology of what has to be
for me. How does anyone else know what you need?
It's more like a derogatory hypocrisy, spreading misery,
projected, in fact, infected, without being asked or elected
to protect, even comes as neglect and disrespect when
someone is telling you what's wrong with you, filling
your head and heart with what doesn't belong to you.
It's a cold truth and an absolute useless move to stay with
anyone who claims they love you, but flat out hurt you.
It's imperative to escape the bonds of the disappointing
narrative. Be true to you and don't compromise
with carelessness on the rarest of gifts.
I ask you this;
if you know time is short, then why would you try to
blend in or settle on being the status quo when
everyone's waiting for your big solo?

Ashes

Some say ashes are just ashes
while others say they're sadness.
They're the remnants of what once was,
the end of a madness, perhaps a sickness.
A past, that happened, that will soon be forgotten.
I too, will be a memory lost in ashes.

But ashes are strength!
he declared in such tone.
Cities are built on top of those old bones,
the phoenix rose from the ashes, not stone.
Dragons thrive on the ash they create
with the inner drive to survive past the death that awaits.
we must carry on with the theme to be great
before we become
the dust of fate.

Printed in the United States
By Bookmasters